Our Story, The Power of Agreement Montage

Copyright © 2019 by Eddie and Davronia Scarbrough

All rights reserved. Except as permitted under the U.S. Copyright Act of 1976, no part of this publication. No part of this book may be reproduced or transmitted in any form or by any means, electronic or mechanical, including photocopying, recording, or by any information storage and retrieval system, without permission in writing from the copyright owner.

ISBN: 978-0-9995498-4-1

Published February 2020

ScarbroughED Publisher

PO Box 29515

Charlotte, NC 28229

Welcome to our World

EDDIE & VAL
THE STORY OF TWO PEOPLE
PUTTING TOGETHER THE PIECES

Val and I have looked forward to the day of sharing our story with the world. On many occasions we have been fortunate enough to share bits and pieces of our story and we have always wanted to bring our love story to one place and pray our story will strengthen, encourage, and even catapult marriages to their next level of reward. So we are overjoyed you took this opportunity to invest in your covenant. Remember, Investment = Increase!

We do a marriage retreat called 'Power of Agreement" which we founded in 1999 and in planning that time of enrichment with couples we always have one thought in mind, and that's to share concepts, truths, and principles that are designed to bring God glory in your union. We have this saying, "our desire is that our marriage is a trophy in the hands of God." We call it "Award Winning Marriage". We understand the struggles of balancing home, careers, children and a relationship. Over the past 28+ years we have discovered the art to growing a healthy relationship in the midst of noises and just know it takes work and investment.

Every time a couple takes time to adjust their lives or take finances to invest in making their covenant stronger and more complete it is time and money well spent. Our marriages need guidance and wisdom and that should never be negotiable. Val and I are always looking for ways to keep us and our relationship healthy & spicy. The time we dedicated to putting this booklet together is time we believe has been well invested, in fact, we think, it's invaluable. We have declared that this book will make a mark in your covenant (marriage) that will last until death do the two of you part.

We look forward to your love testimonies!

Eddie & Val

TABLE OF CONTENTS

01
OUR STORY

02
MARRIAGE FROM A BIBLICAL PERSPECTIVE

03
CAN YOU HEAR ME NOW

04
FAIR FIGHTING

05
TENSION "THE SILENT KILLER"

06
ADAM WHERE ARE YOU?

07
BEING LOYAL TO OUR COVENANT

08
THE EVE SYNDROME

09
THE POWER OF SPICE

10
EVALUATE US!

11
THE RESOLUTION

Our
STORY

THE TRUTH ABOUT OUR STORY

He who finds a wife finds what is good and receives favor from the LORD.
Proverbs 18:22(NIV)

THE DAY I MET HER

The day I met her I had no clue I would be with her some twenty-nine years later. It was a beautiful day as I can recall. I don't think there was a cloud in the sky. It seems as though God set it up so we could see each other clearly. Believe it or not, my mother introduced us to each other. The greeting was as pleasant as a gentle breeze on a spring day. As she and my mother began to walk away from me God synchronized our necks to swivel at the same time and slightly glance back at each other. Wow, what a strange feeling we both would discover later we were having. Not in a lustful way. Just that internal conversation with ourselves that said "that was strange" & "what was that all about"! LOL!! Little did I know that day would change the whole course of my life for the better.

Life with Val has been the greatest adventure of my life!

Spending Life With Her Has Been A Gratifing Adventure!!

That day didn't just change the course of my life, little did I know that day would give me a reason for life! For that I am eternally grateful!

On the day "I met Val", time stood still and allowed us to step into our destiny.

It was almost like waiting in the lobby of a building and pushing the elevator call button only to have the elevator door pop open and give you calculated seconds to step in. We all know that elevator doors close in just a few seconds of opening. I'm so glad I was in the right place at the appropriate time to step on one of the greatest elevators of my life. If I had missed the elevator that day I would have gladly taken the stairs to pursue my girl. Life with her has been such an awesome reality for me. Thank you Jesus!!

The day I met Val heaven set me up for my life today! The thing is, I had been praying for what seemed like eternity for God to hook me up with one of his favorite daughters. Prayers answered because He did exactly what my heart was desiring. Glory to God!

She is the smartest, most intelligent, classy, loving and let's not forget "FINEST" woman I know. God was sho'nuff good to me that day. He allowed me to find her. My life is so full of grace and favor because of her according to Proverbs 18:22 that states " He who finds a wife finds a good thing, and obtains favor from the Lord". Well, I will say this "that's the whole truth and nothing but the truth concerning "The Day I Met Her"!

P.S. GRATEFUL!!!!!!!!!!!!!.

I LOVE HOW SHE MINISTERS TO THE KING IN ME.

THE TRUTH ABOUT OUR STORY

THE DAY I MET HIM

Divine Connections aren't always brought together with music playing in the background and slow motion running into each other's arms. In our case our ordained connection was brought together by someone else seeing and recognizing "The two of you would be great together". THAT'S OUR STORY. Someone else saw our destiny even when the both of us weren't looking.

Life can be funny. You wake up one day not expecting anything extraordinary to happen, you just expect that day to be just like any other day of your life. You start your normal routine, wash your face, brush your teeth, decide what you will wear and plan out your day according to the scope of your life. For me, I had no idea in a few hours after my awakening to greet a normal day... I would meet the man that would change my life forever. I did not start that day off looking for a man to change my life. I did not start that day off looking for my life to be changed at all. However unbeknown to me heaven had a totally different path for me to take. The day that I met Eddie everything would change!

However, each one of you also must love his wife as he loves himself, and the wife must respect her husband.
Ephesians 5:33 (NIV)

The thing is, If you were to ask me what I was doing 3-hours before we met, I would say "I haven't a clue". I only vividly remember 30-mins before our lives ran smack into each other.

It Was a Fall Day In October and

My husband's mother (which was a friend of mine) wanted to go to Captain D's for lunch, so I obliged. I drove across town to pick her u, and as we left her house, she asked, me a question "Do you mind taking me to take my baby some candy?" I said "sure I will".

When we arrived at his location he was outside washing cars. (you would have to know our full story) I pulled into a park in downtown Tuscaloosa, AL in my 1989 Navy Blue Ponitac 6000 and waited for her to exit the car. She said to me "you not coming"? I hesitantly obliged, because saying No would have gotten some backlash. (you would have to know my mother-in-love to understand why I say that) (lol)

My mother-in-love said to her son "Mod" (which she so fondly called him) this is Val. We spoke and that was the gest of our meeting. The magical part of the meeting wasn't when we said hello, it happened at the oddest time, it happened upon our departure from one another. To this day, we both always say how amazing that moment was. As I was walking away, simultaneously we turn around and locked eyes and stared at each other like, hmmm, that was different. Our stare wasn't a lust stare, nor an oooh she fine stare, but like, "that was different" stare.

We didn't exchange numbers or any thing that day, just a friendly hello. We gave no gestures that would indicate any relationship interest at all. A few weeks later my husband was turning 21 and I felt inspired to send him a card, remember, I haven't spoken to him since a few weeks prior when we simply said "Hello".

When I met my husband, I was on this quest to know God better, I had rededicated my life to Christ 10 months earlier and so my focus was to get closer to Jesus. I had returned to being celibate, so you know I was trying to steer clear. Don't get me wrong, I wanted a companion but I had placed a fleece before God and one of them was, "Father, I want a man that will love you the way I love you and will love me the way he loves you". At the time, Eddie had rededicated his life to Christ and was attending church on a regular basis. This was unbeknown to me at the time of our Hello. Long story short, I had been praying for him since December 31 of that previous year because I knew I wanted something meaningful and I wanted a relationship that would please God.

I want to share two instances I questioned God

about our relationship. The first time is when we established we wanted to date. I knew in my heart I wanted to be married, not just date. So, I ask God, Father is this man my husband? One July night we went to the house of a prophet and as we walked to the door she said, "the Lord told me you all would come tonight".

On that night, she laid hands on my husband, then boyfriend, and he was baptized in the holy spirit. As he was crying and praying, she looked at me and said "You asked the Lord was this your husband? And the Lord said "yes". From that moment on regardless of what we faced, I held on to that word…The Lord said "Yes".

The second time I questioned God about our relationship was the day of our wedding. I was standing in the doorway of the church getting ready to walk down the isle and I whispered to the Lord "Father, is this union blessed?" No one heard me say it I literally whispered it.

Well, on our 1st Anniversary we were sitting in our bed reading the word of God together and the phone rang, yep, it was that same lady. She had never called our home before, never reached out to us before, but there she was on our phone.

I answered the phone and she asked "Is your husband near you"? I said "Yes, Ma'am". She said "put him on the phone with us". When he got on the phone the only thing she said was "Daughter, you asked the Lord was this union blessed and the Lord said "Yes".

Have we had our share of ups and downs? Sure we have. Have we had to navigate some difficult waters? Yes. We both wore life-jackets. Nevertheless, one thing we both know for sure is this….We got a word from the Lord and his "Yes" over our union has overridden every demonic attack the enemy has thrown our way. God's "yes" has been the bond to keeping us together.

Almost 30 years later, I have a true revelation of "What God has joined, let no man put asunder".

The Day I Met Him Was Nothing Less Than Heaven Kissing Earth On My Behalf!

OUR STORY "THE POWER OF AGREEMENT"

Relationship Movement

What keeps a relationship moving?
Answer: Apply simple principles

- Communicate (even about hard things)
- Patience (apply it always)
- Compassion (always view your mate from the standpoint, I want to be treated this way)
- Trust (deposit trust frequently)
- Unconditional love
- Sex (connection keeps the heart soft towards one another)
- Affirmation (you should be the biggest cheerleader for your mate)

How we relate to one another can give life to a healthy, lasting, productive, successful relationship.
You can have a dream marriage!

Just do the work and apply the principles.

Marriage Frm A Biblical
PERSPECTIVE

MARRIAGE FROM
A BIBLICAL PERSPECTIVE

THE INTENT

To understand the biblical perspective of marriage there must be an understanding of the intent of God concerning covenant. The biblical perspective of marriage is when two human souls become one...emotionally, spiritually, and physically.

The "Intent" of God is to show forth how Jesus and the church should be viewed here in the earth. Marriage is a beautiful expression of total agreement. The intent of God is for two people to become emotionally, spiritually one, and physically one. For this to happen there must be a willingness to submit one to another "for the greater good of the whole", this is what makes a successful marriage.

A successful union agrees that the goal is to have "unity", if they are to see progression.

The intent of God for marriage was, I will put two people together and they will become one in every way to show forth the great unity of the God-head. In other words, marriage is the picture created by God to show there can be "unity" in humanity. What's the purpose of us becoming "One"?

Unity exemplifies God's way of doing things.
Unity is a kingdom principle.
Unity is the representation of heaven's one accordness.

God's intent for marriage was to take two people made in his image and his likeness and develop single vision just like the Father, Son, and the Holy Spirit.
This is why he said "Let us make man in our image, and in our likeness and let "Them"(this unified body) have dominion.

The Successful Marriage Equation

**Husband + Wife + Holy Spirit =
Jesus in the Midst
The father is
looking to increase a unified nation. I Corn
1:10-13**

Marriage is a covenant that should have a universal language. Having the word of God being the final authority within the marriage. Genesis 11:1-6

You have to create the language you want to speak in your marriage, your nation. Example: We came speaking different languages concerning finances, house keeping, child rearing, and conflict resolution. Concerning those issues we came speaking Scarbrough & Dunnigan's language, the two languages were different. So, we had to create our own ABC's & 123's so that agreement could take place in the nation we were creating.

MARRIAGE FROM
A BIBLICAL PERSPECTIVE

IMPROVING THE IMPAIRMENTS

You may be asking what does impairments have to do with a "Biblical Perspective"? We are glad you asked. Impairments are malfunctions that can stop or hold up manifestations in a marriage.

Many couples are believing God for things but because there are some malfunctions, things are not manifesting.

Here are a few things that can cause a lack of manifestation in marriages.

A.   Idol Worship – money, careers, children, time, etc...
Ex 34:10-17
(We have found over the years many couples have set up idols unbeknowning.)

Cont.

B.   Selfishness - selfishness comes to suffocate a the marriage.

C.   Pettiness – is when insecurity and immaturity overshadows sound communication within the relationship.

D.   Lack of Commitment – your word and your actions reflects a single mind & heart and not a unified mind & hear. These are impairments that stop manifestations.

THE LANGUAGE OF AN AWARD WINNING MARRIAGE SOUNDS DIFFERENT!

I Protect You –
Ephesian 5:25 & 28-29

I Sacrifice For You
Ephesian 5:1-2

I Give Time To Us
Mark 14:14-15

We Educate Ourselves
Ephesian 5:26

I Submit Freely
Ephesian 5:21-25

THERE IS A LANGUAGE TO AN AWARD WINNING MARRIAGE

An extraordinary marriage is when the "two have become one" in heart, thoughts, actions, and words!

Can You Hear Me NOW

THE POWER OF AGREEMENT - "OUR STORY"

CAN YOU HEAR ME NOW

The Passion To Communicate

The Passion To Communicate

There has to be a desire on both parties to have effective and affective communication in the marriage.

Embrace The Following:

a. Expressing Myself – Proverbs 13:12
b. Fighting Fare – Proverbs 16:27
c. Actively Listen -James 1:19 & Prov. 18:13
d. Your Opinion Matters
e. Never Demean Your Spouse - Proverbs 21:2

Money Matters!

Money is a huge communicator in a marriage. How you manage it can affect the way you relate to one another.

Proverbs 13:22

WITHOUT A DESIRE TO HAVE PRODUCTIVE COMMUNICATION YOU ALL WILL END UP NOWHERE!

Marriage Communication:

UNDERSTANDING THE ELEMENTS OF COVENANT COMMUNICATION

COMMUNICATION
(THE KEY TOO A SUCCESSFUL MARRIAGE)

Communication – The act of communicating; transmission.

Successful Communication in marriage takes the following:

a. The exchange of thoughts, information, with appropriate speech and/or behavior.

b. Interpersonal rapport

c. Developing techniques that are productive in the exchange of information or ideas within your marriage.

Questions For You As A Couple:

1. Does your covenant have effective communication skills? (Proverbs 15:23)

2. Does your communication exemplify wisdom when speaking to your spouse? (Proverbs 15:1-7)

3. Are you honest in your communicating? (Proverbs 26:28)

4. Are you accountable for the words you speak in your covenant? (Matthews 12:33-37)

Fair Fighting...

CONFLICT RESOLUTION SHOULD BE HEALTHY AND PRODUCTIVE

Rule I – Know your strengths

Rule II – Admit your weakness to your mate. (It's easier than you think to say "sweetheart, that's a weakness for me") TRY IT!

Rule III – Never use your mate's weakness to gain control.

Rule IV – Never play the blame game, be accountable for your actions.

Rule V – Never use words that are permanent: like; "you never", "you always", "you don't", & "you can't". When we make permanent statements we weaken our belief in the power of God to change our circumstance.

Tension The Silent KILLER

TENSION: THE SILENT KILLER

What causes tension?
How can tension kill my marriage?
How can we identify tension in our marriage?

We are so glad you asked us those questions?

Over the years of counseling and yes, even in our own marriage "Tension" has tried to take us out.

We want to share a story that caused us to identify and pay close attention to the silent killer called tension. One year(2006) we were faced with a lot of huge financial decisions.

When we tell you everything was going wrong, we mean everything.

Our cars had died, our home mortgage was rising monthly (we bought a home during the time of the housing boom under some crazy terms...long story), our business was loosing money and the church only had about 20-members at the time if that many. When we say everything was going awry that's an understatement.

We were barely talking and when we did you would have thought we were mortal enemies. There was so much tension in our home that neither one of us wanted to come home or talk with each other.

Let us be clear no couple should ever live like this.

**FACT
The Unspoken
Can
Speak Louder
Than
What's Being Said!**

We did not get married to live in an environment that is so hostile that we regret the happiest day of our lives.

We allowed tension to build up in our home to the degree we both knew it was slowly killing a marriage we knew was ordained by God and it was killing our respect for one another.

Tension is a silent killer!

Most problems that are found in marriages are due to miscommunication. Tension thrives on miscommunication!

We found during pressured times your marriage can drown in the pool of tension unnecessarily all due to miscommunicating.

Why do we say unnecessarily? We say this because as a couple you can simply defeat tension by standing up and communicating your feelings. We found that we were dealing with some emotions separately concerning the financial situation we were facing. We were dealing with hurt, disappointments, discouragement, and we both were feeling as if we fail one another.

So, we started looking at tension like this, "many people tend to drown in shallow water simply because their minds have convinced them the water is deeper than what it really is" when all you have to do is stand up! When we admitted, hey, there has been some miscommunication lately and our transmitters have been off. We then started to defeat tension.

So this is what we did. One day we put our marriage on a fast just to get our communication back in line.

What do you mean put the marriage on a fast. Well, we decided to withhold sex for 30-days, we made a conscious decision to unpack everything facing us and talk clearly and intentionally about those things and our feelings about what was going on.

In those 30-days we dealt with little nuisances that had turned into mountains, but most of all we developed this thing we do to this day. We will intentionally say "How did you hear that"?

We do it all the time! That season taught us this valuable lesson that "Tension is a silent killer, but we decided our marriage wasn't going to die.
Contribution: "VS"

Tension The Silent Killer!

The first thing that comes to my mind when I hear the word tension is things become tight. When things get tight there is resistance. One of the reasons tension is a silent killer is because most couples tend to shut down all forms of communication. This is a big NO NO in your covenant because communication is a very much needed component to having an award winning marriage.

When tension enters a marriage its like committing suicide. You can find yourself sucking the life out of your own union by catering to the spirit of stubbornness. Be determined to be the one to initiate an act of peace. I guess what we are trying to say is don't give the devil a foot hold in your relationship.

POWER OF AGREEMENT

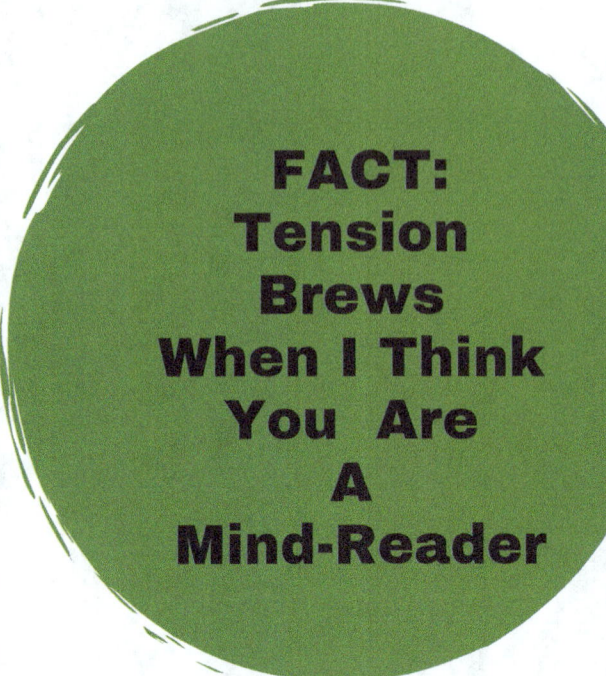

FACT: Tension Brews When I Think You Are A Mind-Reader

We have to keep him out by any means necessary! His number one job is to divide and conquer. Jesus said it best in scripture "If a kingdom is divided against itself, that kingdom cannot stand. And if a house is divided against itself, that house cannot stand" (Mark 3:24-25

The will of God is for your marriage to stand against any and all kinds of test and trials. Be determined to love respect and honor your spouse so tension can't creep in and destroy what God has joined together.

Lets talk a little bit about the art of apologizing. We have learned over the years to be quick to apologize to each other even if we were not the one to commit the offense

This is what you call taking the high road. Taking the low road is easy because it takes the lease amount of effort. Keeping tension out of your home and marriage will always take work on both of your part. Marriage is a partnership that should never be broken especially by that demonic spirit called tension. Be determined to keep everything light between you and your spouse and when you do you will literally destroy tension the silent killer.

Contributor: "ES"

"Chaos will muzzle the voice of reason"

POWER OF AGREEMENT

Every time "Pride" is destroyed Your Marriage Is Rejuvenated

Adam
Where Are
YOU?

I HAVE TO REMIND MYSELF "EDDIE CONTINUE TO BE AVAILABLE..."

ADAM WHERE ARE YOU?
STAY ON POST!

dam Where Are You?
Husbands one thing that we have to understand is that God has called us to be the leaders of our home and family. This was actually the plan of God from the beginning of time. Not to be domineering or controlling but to be responsible. Yes I said responsible! As the head of our home and family we should be accountable for what takes place among the people that are under our covering. You see we have a call on our life to watch over and cover our wives and children. After all we were the first image of God created here in the earth although everything came out of God. Hallelujah, what an honor! God is a coverer. And He put those same attributes in us And they heard the sound of the LORD God walking in the garden in the cool of the day and Adam and his wife hid themselves from the presence of the LORD God among the trees of the garden.

Then the LORD God called to Adam and said to him, "Where are you? (Genesis 3:8-9 NKJV)
If you noticed God did not say Eve where are you. Why? Because God knew that if He could locate Adam He would locate Eve. Where ever Adam is Eve should be there also; often times we can tend to put our responsibilities off on our wives as well as our children. This is totally out of order! One example is something I heard years ago. When you see a Mother and her children going to church that's a good thing. But when you see a Husband, wife and children going to church that's a family. This is absolutely the truth. If you are a husband or believing God to become one we must understand and adjust to the task as hand. We are called and created to lead.

Being an absentee husband isn't the definition of being a great husband. We should be readily available and always willing to be located when needed.

POWER OF AGREEMENT

Adam was the first initiator of the blame game. As a husband accountability is very, very important in a marriage. When a husband allows things to get out of control that's when the spirit of divorce can creep in.

> "There should never be a time where God or our spouse should have to search for us."

You may be saying to yourself, I've messed up as a husband! I haven't been doing what is expected or required of me! I have great news for you. Start now! Get a fresh start. Acknowledge your slackness, repent and move on. You see, once we face these short comings. We can start to rebuild and be present from this moment forward. We can't allow pride to keep us from being found. Pride will make you hide. Every time pride is destroyed your marriage is rejuvenated

Pride is the greatest danger to a relationship, especially a marriage. Pride is what caused Adam not to take responsibility for his actions in the garden of eden.

I truly believe if Adam had taken responsibility and not shifted the blame on Eve, God would have forgiven them. Wow! Could it be that the fall of mankind happened because of a lack of repentance from Adam or accountability? Really Adam!!!!

Think about it, the only question God asked Adam was, Adam where are you?

I believe 100% of the failures in homes are because Adam can't be found.

THE POWER OF AGREEMENT

BEING LOYAL TO OUR COVENANT

IT'S NOT A DREAM FOR US IT IS OUR LIFE

Loyalty To Our "I Do"

LOYALTY

What does it mean to be Loyal to your covenant or to your marriage?

Loyalty is greater than sexual fidelity. However, being loyal to your spouse with your body is what is expected and required when you said "I Do".

On the other hand, we want to dig a little deeper into loyalty regarding marriage as a whole.

We want to identify some Loyalty traits that should be established in our union to insure an "Award Winning Marriage".

1. I must treat my spouse with human dignity.
2. Loyalty is protecting your spouses heart. Genesis 39:7-9
3. Loyalty is walking in integrity when I am not with my spouse. Psalms 26:1-2
4. I remain "Loyal" even when conditions aren't favorable or deserves my loyalty.
5. Loyalty is setting standards that I live by when I am seen by others or not being seen by others. Proverbs 10:9-10
6. Loyalty is having a navigational system established to help us nurture marital success. Proverbs 11:3
7. Loyalty isn't fair-weather.
8. I am loyal to our covenant even when being loyal isn't popular.
9. I know my spouse depends on my loyalty, even if I am tempted to be disloyal.
10. My Loyalty is rooted in "I dare not break the heart that has entrusted me to fulfill my words until death do us part".

An "Award Winning Marriage" is committed to "Loyalty". Award Winning couples know at all times these basic things should be in place or progressing towards these goals.

We believe a long-lasting marriage is built by two people who believe in -and live by- the solemn promise they made to be "loyal" to each other and to the vow they made before a cloud of witnesses.

Our "I Do" Deserves 100% Loyalty

THE POWER OF AGREEMENT

THE GIFT OF YOU!

We have agreed that "change" is always good when its for the health of the marriage. However, when a person desires one to change to become what they want this is a selfish ambition. (a version of themselves in a different body)

Nothing healthy ever comes out of selfishness.

Award Winning Marriages know pinpointing areas that need strengthening in the marriage is not a statement that something is wrong with either one of us, at least, not to the degree we have to become our spouse to be a better version of ourselves.

If your opinion of "change" is to challenge your spouse to become another version of you; are you really getting the gift of who they are and what they bring to your life?
To think the greatest version of our spouse is for them to become a version of "us", in another human suit, is simply stating "I want to be married to myself with the benefits of sex from you". That's a cheap gift!

Award Winning Marriages realize their spouse is an extremely valuable gift given to them by God for the benefit of making the "marriage" a beautiful gift to the both of them.

LOYALTY IS NEVER "SELFISH"

In Award Winning Marriages both people cherish every day they can wake up to build confidence in their spouse; because they understand that difficult times will come and it is of great value to them to have built a "mental highway" that will sustain their love in the curves of life.

THE POWER OF AGREEMENT

OUR STORY "THE POWER OF AGREEMENT"
Couples

Couples tend to think if there is a disagreement or if they don't see eye-to-eye they are not meant to be together or in many cases they tend to think they have fallen out of love. Love is not constituted on if you agree with your spouse's opinion, ideas, or even the way they handle day-to-day situations. Love is based on the commitment of the heart to be committed to your union regardless of opinions. When you live from this place of "commitment" it makes life with your spouse more enjoyable.

The Scarbroughs' will say this, when there is agreement within your union the power of forgiveness, tolerance, and patience is greater and things tend to run smoother. There will be a peace that will rest within the union. Nonetheless, a lack of agreement doesn't mean that you aren't compatible, it only means you have to develop ways to stand on common grounds (that takes being ok with surrendering your right to be right).

Remember, opinions change like the weather; because opinions are based on the facts presented at the time.

Our love and commitment (The Scarbroughs') to our union makes this statement on a daily basis. "Despite a lack of understanding at times, despite days of not seeing eye-to-eye, we can't see ourselves doing life with anyone else but each other".

When a couple resolves in their hearts the above-statement, it takes no, it removes the pressure of "You always feeling the need to be right" (in other words stop majoring in the minor things just to be right). Living in peace should mean more to you than a minute in time of one needing to be right.

In short, don't allow something temporal to wreck the commitment made to one another "one minute in time"...you have to ask yourself which minute in time is more valuable to you?

The Eve SYNDROME

THE EVE SYNDROME

JUST BECAUSE...

*JUST BECAUSE I HAVE BEEN GIVEN DOMINION, POWER & AUTHORITY. MY GREATEST STRENGTH IS MY RESPECT FOR YOU, ADAM

*JUST BECAUSE I CAN SEE DOESN'T MEAN I DON'T RESPECT YOUR VISION

*JUST BECAUSE I CAN HEAR DOESN'T MEAN I DISCOUNT YOUR VOICE!

*JUST BECAUSE I CAN BUY THE FIELD DOESN'T MEAN I BYPASS YOUR OPINION ABOUT THE FIELD!

VAL JUST BECAUSE YOU CAN, SHOULD YOU?

So many times I have taught on the Eve syndrome and how wrong communication and the effects of it caused Adam and Eve to be foreclosed upon and kicked out of their dream home. It's hard to admit but the snowball effect started with Eve gambling with her position. (gamble means: take risky action in the hope of a desired result) I have found in many marriages we gamble with our position as wives hoping to get a result that benefits us and not the whole. The bible tells us in Proverbs 14:1 "The wise woman builds her house, but the foolish pulls it down with her own hands". When I use to read that I would always think, "how does she pull her house down with her own hands"? Then one day it hit me, she pulls down her own house with her actions and communication.

How a wife presents things to her husband makes a world of difference in how he responds to a situation or circumstance. Presentation is everything! So often I pray, how to present something to Eddie, because I know if the presentation is off, it can cause him to "Go Off"! Eve was an influencer, you are an influencer. Eve is a master communicator, she can twist it, spin it, pretty it up or drama it up to get the outcome "she desires". So because of this Eve syndrome, my question to myself constantly is, "Just because I can, should I"?

Presentation Is Everything!

Eve had an great relationship with God and her husband until she was introduced to evil communication. This is why as married women we have to guard ourselves from evil communication.

You may ask how do you know they had a great relationship? Well, its absolutely obvious Adam was not intimidated by her, we can clearly see he didn't have a problem with her intelligence and he trusted her judgement; because he didn't try to interfere with her conversation. Sounds like a good relationship to me. Trust, respect, space, yep they had a good relationship So, you ask me, then what is the problem? The problem is, she abused her position of influence and her seat of authority in Adam's life. Before she had wrong communication or communication outside of her marriage, things were good. Adam trusted Eve to keep their relationship from any outside influences.

The bible tells us in Proverbs 31:11 "The heart of her husband safely trusts her; so he will have no lack of gain."

In other words, the most guarded part of a man, his heart, is only given to the woman he trust.

When a man trust a woman with his heart, he is making the statement "I am trusting you with a part of me that I saved just for you".

I find that to be an awesome honor Eddie has bestowed upon me, yep, I said bestowed. He trust me with his heart.

This is why I watch my presentation.

In the past when I have taught this I would get my sista's rolling their eyes and shaking their heads all because they would think I am coming against the woman, but I am not. Eve had some issues...Point-Blank-Period!

This is why we have to be real and deal with this syndrome. We are asking Adam to deal with his shortcomings but we put sugar & make-up on ours.

Nope, shouldn't be!

How do we kill this syndrome? Simple, Eve watch your conversations and your presentation!

The Power of SPICE

THE POWER OF SPICE...
Parmesan Cheese
KICK IT UP A NOTCH!!

Over the years of pastoring and having the privilege of counseling couples, we have observed a pattern in marriages experiencing staleness or marriages that are navigating through serious waters. We have come to the conclusion, there is a common thread that unravels before we are brought into the picture. They stop exploring and discovering things about each other. As our desires, needs, and views change, we change. What may have been interesting to us in our 20's may not hold great value when you are 40. As a couple, we've taken time to always find out what is of interest to each other in the season we are in; because in reality no one likes things that are stale. (I.e. potato chips, bread, your home, etc..). When things are stale the first thought that comes to mind is "discard" and replace with something fresher/newer. Due to that very knowledge this is why we are always finding joy in pursuing moments of "discovery".

We believe there should always be a constant conversation on ways and ideas to "kick it up a notch". We call it the Parmesan Cheese affect! (Because we all know, Parmesan cheese takes a dish to another level and sends our mouth on a happy dance.)

Discovery can happen in any area of your marriage, for instance, the way you resolve conflict, the way you plan vacations, the way you drive to your favorite restaurant, the way you engage in intimacy, etc.. . You learn so much about your spouse when you invite the language of discovery into your marriage. Recently, we were on a trip to a place we frequent often; nonetheless, we ventured off the beaten path and discovered homes, landscaping, and towns we had never visited.

Our agreement to venture off the beaten path opened up finding out something new about one another on that trip(no we are not going to tell you what we found out about one another...lol). Bottom-line, never get to a place where you don't want to know any more about your spouse! Set your hearts to continue to "Discover" more about each other so things don't become stale. Be determined to set your marriage up to "**Kick it up a Notch**".

#DiscoveryZone   #ExplorationCanBeFunandExciting   #AwardWinningMarriages
#KeepItFresh   #Getting2KnowYouMoreandMore   #SeverTheStaleness

UNITY BRINGS THE SPICE TO LIFE!

Marriage is real life and not to be taken lightly or treated as if it is Fantasy Island. Nor should it be treated like a toxic waste field.

You may be asking us what does unity have to do with spicing up the marriage? It has everything to do with keeping the spice in a marriage. Without unity there will be no desire to spice up things or to discover each other. Unity is the foundation of spice. Until there is a sense of one accord, or movement to be on one accord, our marriages run the risk of unraveling. Unity kicks the marriage up 3-notches!

Why Is Unity Important To Our Marriage?

- Unity unifies a "Vision" (bring us together to accomplish one common goal).
- Our Unity exemplifies the kingdom of God.
- Unity is the greatest kingdom principle we can display in our marriage.
- When you sow discord the "devil has a foothold in your marriage.
- Unity empowers the anointing upon our marriage.
- Marriage can not survive under the pressure of separatism.
- The spirit of "Unity" has a single eye (The power of God always invades a places that is unified). Act 2:1-4
- Unity is the courier of spice.

THE POWER OF AGREEMENT

OUR STORY "THE POWER OF AGREEMENT"

Vulnerability

The Importance of Vulnerability

What does it mean to be vulnerable? The definition of "Vulnerable" is: open to attack, harm or damage.

When our spouse makes the decision to be vulnerable, they are saying " I've counted the cost and I am willing to open up to you at the cost of possibly being hurt. It is also an emotional statement "I am handing you a precious treasure (my vulnerability) because "I trust you with me". For our spouse to make the emotional statement "I trust you with me" that's nothing to be taken lightly. Genesis 2:25 (NLT) Now the man and his wife were both naked, but they felt no shame. Bottom line, when there is a lack of being vulnerable or an uneasiness about being vulnerable, it is a statement "I only trust you so far with me". In an Award Winning Marriage one thing we should remember, is to never take our spouse's emotional and mental state for granted. Take a few moments and ask yourself these questions. (1.) Can you be trusted with your spouse's vulnerabilities? (2.) Do you feel comfortable exposing your vulnerabilities to your spouse? (3.) Are you willing to handle your spouse's vulnerabilities with kit-gloves (compassion, love, tenderness & understanding).

Last but not least, just know when we cover our emotional vulnerabilities it builds up invisible walls that can cause hinderances in our marriage that will affect communication, family structure, trust, intimacy, goals and dreams.

Hey, take a moment and do what we did, rate your vulnerability on a scale of 1-10
If you rated yourself:
1-3 - Open up more, push past the zone of being uncomfortable
4-6 - You are on the right track, keep pushing forward
7-10 - You are in a good place, continue to knock it out of the park

#CanITrustYouWithMe

Evaluate US!

Key: (1) Rarely or Never (2) Sometimes (3) Often (4) Almost Always

EVALUATE WHERE WE ARE   1 - 4

1. Do You Hold Each Other Accountable? _____
2. My Spouse Cares About My Feelings _____
3. Respects me & my opinions _____
4. Protects and defends me _____
5. Encourages me to be the best I can be, and is supportive even when I make mistakes _____
6. Engages with me in meaningful conversations and really "hears" me _____
7. Puts my needs above his/her own
8. Finds me physically attractive and tells me so _____
9. Enjoys spending time with me _____
10. Expresses much love and passion in our sex life _____

TOTAL _____

- 36-48: You are loving and respecting each other well
- 28-35: Things are good but could be even better•

27 or Below: You have work to do, but take heart, your best days could be ahead

Key: (1) Aggressively (2) Even-Tempered (3) Passive
(4) Overly-Excited

HEAVENLY SEX!   1 - 4

1. When you express your feelings are you? _____

2. When you prepare for sex do you prepare your spouse mind and emotions? _____

3. Do you engage in foreplay? YES__ N__

4. Are you considerate of your spouse's feelings when it comes to the act of sex? YES____ NO____

5. Do you know how to make your wife have an orgasm? YES____ NO___

6. Is it your desire to make your wife climax before the end of your sexual encounters? YES____ NO____

7. Do you explore your spouse's body YES____ NO____ or just go for it?

The important discussion every couple should have when it comes to love-making

- Do you know if you are completely satisfying your spouse?
- Am I kissing you enough to make you feel wanted by me?
- Do you need me to hug you more or am I doing ok?
- Do I flirt with you enough to keep the spark and interest in our love affair?
- What more can I do energize our love-making?

We Desire To See

THIS HAPPEN IN OUR RELATIONSHIP...

_____
_____
_____
_____
_____
_____
_____
_____
_____
_____
_____
_____
_____
_____

Our
RESOLUTION

The Marriage Vows From A

BIBLICAL RESOLUTION

IN THE SIGHT OF GOD. 1 JOHN 5:6-8

IN HOLY MATRIMONY. GENESIS 2:21-25

WHICH IS AN HONORABLE INSTITUTION... EPHESIANS 5:25-27

HONORABLE & THE BED UNDEFILED. HEBREW 13:4

I REQUIRE AND CHARGE YOU BOTH. EPHESIANS 5:11-13

GOD'S HOLY ORDINANCES. MARK 10:1-7

Today I_____ and I_____ commit to our wedding vows and will remain loyal to our covenant. We will allow the word of God to be the final authority in our marriage covenant ONLY!
We commit to God this day our marriage and declare our union will be a trophy
for the "Kingdom Of God".
No weapon formed against our covenant will ever
prosper. Money, sex, lies, nor people will ever put us asunder.

IN JESUS NAME. AMEN.

OUR STORY "THE POWER OF AGREEMENT"

We Speak Life

Into your marriage

We thank you for allowing us to speak into your marriage covenant through these pages. We pray that something has been released through our words, concepts and openness that will fortify your marriage even the more. We know it can be hard for couples to look things directly in the eye and change old patterns; however, we believe that this book has been set in the earth for such a time as this.

We speak health, wholeness, love, passion, forgiveness, compassion, brotherly love towards each other and declare what God has joined together let no man/woman put asunder.

We bind every force of divorce that comes to steal your fruit, joy, peace, understanding, and love. We bind the spirit of divorce and give charge to the warring angels that have been assigned to your union, to war against every demonic assignment formed.

May the two of you enjoy the remaining of your days in earth as a beautiful representation of "A Trophy" in the hands of God.

OUR STORY "THE POWER OF AGREEMENT"

Make Some Notes Of What You Would Like To See In Your Marriage From This Day Forward...

www.ingramcontent.com/pod-product-compliance
Lightning Source LLC
Chambersburg PA
CBHW060428010526
44118CB00017B/2402